TANKA : WAKA : UTA

EXPLORATIONS
IN FORMS OF JAPANESE VERSE

by

Hayashi

MUDBORN PRESS • 2015

Tanka Waka Uta, Hayashi (Dennis Holt) copyright © 2015 Mudborn Press
ISBN 978-0-930012-67-0

BETA BOOKS

The Family Secret, Last American Housewife, Period Pieces, Eleanore Hill

SHAKESPEARE DIRECTORS PLAYBOOK SERIES

Hamlet   Merchant of Venice Twelfth Night   Romeo and Juliet
Taming of the Shrew   A Midsummer Night's Dream   Henry V
As You Like It   Richard III   Much Ado About Nothing   Othello
Macbeth   Antony and Cleopatra   King Lear Julius Caesar

HISTORY

Mitos y Leyendas/Myths and Legends of Mexico (Bilingual)
The Beechers Through the 19th Century
Uncle Tom's Cabin, Harriet Beecher Stowe
The Deserted Village, Ossian, Babylonian Captivity

SCHOOLING AND LANGUAGE

Don't Panic: Procrastinator's Guide to Writing a Term Paper
First Person Intense   Art of Writing (Stevenson)
How to Write... (Poe)   How to Tell a Story (Twain)
How to See a Play (Burton)   Write it Right (Bierce)
The Gospel According to Tolstoy   Gandhi on the Gita
The Everlasting Gospel, Blake   Italian for Opera Lovers
French for Food Lovers   Doctorese for the imPatient
Yiddish, You Say. Nu?   Deadword Dictionary   Ghazals of Ghalib

TEACHERS ONLY

(Q & A, glossaries, critical comments)
Areopagitica   Apology of Socrates, & Crito   Sappho
Leaves of Grass (1855), Whitman   Uncle Tom's Cabin, H.B. Stowe

OTHER

The First Detective: 3 Stories. Poe   Hadji Murad, Tolstoy
Frankenstein, Mary Shelley   Surfing, Jack London Ski, Doyle
The Martian Testament, Eight 2 Two

Mudborn Press and Beta Books are imprints of Bandanna Books

INTRODUCTION

The tanka (or waka or uta) is a Japanese poetic form of great antiquity. It is believed to have originated as early as the 7th century of the current era & has been the preferred verse-form during much of Japanese literary history since then. Consisting of five lines with a 5-7-5-7-7 syllabic pattern, it is essentially an expanded haiku. However, historically the tanka is earlier, the haiku not having arisen until about the 10th century.

I began composing both types of little poems in English (& sometimes in Spanish) many years ago, with some efforts that I consider quite successful. My own policy & practice in creating these has been to keep to a strict syllabic count as in the Japanese models — playing tennis with a net, as Robert Frost might say. Because English syllables are, on the average, inherently more meaningful than Japanese syllables, this naturally leads to poems that are richer in meaning over all than poems of the same structural type in Japanese. Seen from the other side of things, this also means that translators of Japanese haiku & tanka into English must sometimes pad their lines through wordy circumlocutions if they wish to maintain the original syllable-count in their translations.

A few years ago, my friend Anita Chundak loaned me the book *Crossing State Lines*, a unique sort of anthology of short poems by 52 poets ranged all across "these States" (as the Good Gray

Poet would say) coordinating the composition of their poems in a linked manner, as has been traditional in Japanese literary culture for centuries. The editors of the little volume established an order of transmission for the projected collection & suggested that the standard format for each poem be a double tanka: two tanka(s) one after the other, the two of them sharing a common theme, begun in the first tanka & further developed in the second. Successive poets in the chain were encouraged to link their contribution to the immediately previous one so that a sense of continuity of semantic flow might be established & maintained. However, not every poet in the anthology abided by these prescriptions, some of them seeming to have ignored the semantics of what came before in the chain so as to harp again on well-worn personal themes, while a few others ignored the formal prescription entirely, producing free-form poems that are in no way structurally akin to the tanka.

As I read through the little anthology, I realized that it would not be very difficult at all for me to produce a book a lot like that one, but made up of just my own five- & ten-line compositions. So quite naturally & readily I then shifted a significant amount of my literary attention to the making of such poemlets, & now, just a few years later, I have been able to gather together & present here a sizeable collection of these. Apparently, the rules for composing tanka do not include a prescription for themes out of nature — as is the case with haiku — & thus the subject-matter of these poems ranges quite broadly & all-inclusively.

In contemplating the double tanka that I've produced over the last few years, I have noticed a number of different ways in which the second tanka may relate to the first. In some cases the second part provides a bit of commentary, in more general terms, about what has just been presented in the first part; in other cases more information, at the same level of particularity, is added; while in still other cases a semantically unrelated but temporally co-occurring set of images may be presented.

The poems in this little book are presented in two groups: the single tanka first; then the double tanka. I had originally thought to indicate here also the date of composition of each poem, but I have abandoned that idea in the belief that one of the underlying motivations & intentions of both tanka & haiku is to somehow encapsulate, in just a few syllables, the poignancy of certain particular moments of experience without regard to their overall cultural or historical context. I have come to realize that the quality of any one of these poems depends not merely on the skill of the poet at selecting & organizing the semantic & lexical elements that are to be included, but also, & primarily, on the sheer facts of the original immediate perception.

Hayashi

SINGLE TANKA

I walk home clutching
three giant honey-mushrooms
nobody knows them
no one sees them in the light
along the midnight highway

⊕

four teal ducks & one
so brown she's almost hidden
by the muddy creek —
that yellowish translucence
that may persist for a week

⊕

slim-tipped juniper-
branches seem to seek in one
way, then another:
something's there above them to
find & grasp at in the sky

I throw a party.
For two hours no one comes.
Then a fly shows up.
"Good to have you," I tell him
(sotto voce) as he flies in.

⊕

today I'm lucky:
get this shady parking-spot
under the plum-tree;
next week we should find some nice
new prunes on the roof & hood

⊕

something — who knows what —
caused those gulls to all at once
vacate the sandbar
at which they'd all assembled:
gregariousness on the wing

where there's a willow
there's usually a water-way —
some river or creek
near which to plant one's roots deep:
the course of the life-force

⊕

over night, wild pea-
blooms shrink & lose those bright pink
hues they bear at first
by turning dark purple, dyed
by the deep blue of evening

⊕

two rambunctious crows
start cawing high above me
in the magnolia,
right over my head, where I
come to try to right my head

the squarling sax of
David "Fathead" Newman all
of a sudden blares
out the speakers, & then the
voice of the master himself

⊕

a black-spotted, green-
headed beetle greets me as
I settle by the
river: lifts its elytra &
flies from my finger away

⊕

levees infested
with ground-squirrels; they scurry back
into their nests bored
deep among the granite stones —
not at all arboreal

that dragonfly's wings
are a steady blur as it
hovers over the
muddy river like a live
Catalina patrol-plane

⊕

the rain has now stopped,
yet large drops fall from the leaves
to this notebook page
making small pools of inky
water like tiny lenses

⊕

the old road's still there,
winding among the old oaks
beside the highway
that cuts right across its curves
to San Luis Obispo

October & the
floss-silk-trees are in flower:
huge magenta blooms
in glorious widespread arrays
visible ten blocks away

⊕

this ring of asphalt
curb around the lone redwood
breaks for a drain-grate
there at the east, like a kind
of enzo to welcome dawn

⊕

slicing potatoes
for near future frying, I
seem to hear in the
sounds of the knife-strokes the same
quick question: "What now? What now?"

the pyracantha-
berries glare out as wide swaths
of bright red against
the dark green of the bushes:
it will be a cold winter

⊕

the train's lonesome moans
resound across the center
of the town, drowning
out the traffic-noise for brief,
purely melodious moments

⊕

under the oak-tree
beside the bank, the acorns
fall one by one, each
with a small, acorn-size "thump",
onto the tender green grass

flurries of footsteps
from tiniest dogs: the closest
canine thing to what
hummingbirds & bees do, up
in the air with their furious wings

⊕

blackbirds & starlings
compete for crusts that someone's
thrown in the gutter —
a feeding-frenzy that's quelled
just when people's feet cross there

⊕

those thin rods with their
red & white ribbons extend
the dancer's slim arms
as if the genius of the
atlatl had been turned to peace

cabooselessly the
slow freight disappears into
the dark overpass:
boxcar after boxcar its
colorful graffiti dims

⊕

haze of wood-smoke fills
the glen where Kings Creek meets the
river, then takes on
another reality
as its smell enters the bus

⊕

in a big metal
basin she makes a latte,
carefully carries
it through the open door, &
sets it down for the pony

an early morning
rooster crows a Morse-code "V"
as if praising the
sun for its most recent bright
& victorious arrival

⊕

the very air is
alive with energy there where
the bright hummingbird
stretches out its fine-fledged wings
& fans them so fast they sing!

⊕

tattoos bespeak an
attitude that tends to peak
when a person runs
out of available skin
to keep such images in

fallen autumn leaves
lain long leave pictures of them-
selves on the sidewalk:
like the Shroud of Turin, yet
not so godly incarnate

⊕

the acacias are
purple now with their great gobs
of seed-pods dangling
everywhere where once those bright
yellow flowers had their day

⊕

one odd duck among
a hundred seagulls: don't this
relationship seem
just a little absurd? &
you thought you were a weird bird!

a thick chunk of drift-
wood brought down stream by the spring
rains now lies like a
small Henry Moore sculpture on
these sunlit riverside sands

⊕

so much must depend
on a hueless wheelbarrow
that has left its track
on the muddy path leading
to the feed-trough, then gone back

⊕

as I approached the
ponies skedaddled & ran
to huddle in the
middle of the pasture, while
the cows grazed on unconcerned

a candy-wrapper
I hadn't noticed turns out
to be a bright leaf!
the dark plays tricks on my eyes,
but what cruel expectations!

⊕

in deep blue & gray
the Norton Simon guards all
end their art-filled day:
at six sharp, in one huge group
they troop to where their cars are

⊕

crippled critters come
creeping out of the woodwork
of this weird world to
limp & slither before me,
evoking my sympathy

magnolia-petals
blown down to the ground, browning,
far from their crowning
glory, yet somehow, even
now, their story still goes on

⊕

a spider-web stretched
between two tall trees: beyond
that sheer dream-catcher
the aspirations of millions
keyed to that Kerouac bivouac

⊕

one by one the young
mergansers pop up after
diving together
under the water for what-
ever it is they get there

first that fine perfume:
blossoming plum-trees warmed by
the late winter sun;
then the humming of bees in
their petal-laden branches

⊕

pomegranates split
wide open like big red heads
with gaping mouths &
bloody sweet teeth that keep on
falling till the whole tree's bare

⊕

quiet attention,
where'er you happen to be,
may lead you to see . . .
what I cannot tell — for I
was in a diff'rent deep well

the rims of their wheels
shine like four golden rings as
a father & son
pedal down the levee path
in the late afternoon sun

⊕

the great blue heron
standing stick still at the edge
of the slow river
suddenly strikes! gets a beak
full of writhing sashimi

⊕

ven'rable café,
where the queen of street-poets
sits, & waits, & baits
her latest book with friendly
looks, then takes your bucks & goes

the river flutters
as it flows to the ocean
through this twilight dusk;
the hue of this time is rust;
the cry always is "Freedom!"

⊕

as the bus descends,
the nearby slopes rise up to
mask the view I've had
of a distant ridge-line whose
highest peak vanishes last

⊕

pastures so wide &
fog so dense that it all goes
gray , even before
your eyes arrive at the fence
over on the other side

a person's way of
walking is a gate into
some sense of the soul
that inhabits somehow those
waddling or scurrying shoes

⊕

crowding the air here,
the hub-bub of human talk:
Friday afternoon
at the pub in the mountains,
where so much is now flowing

⊕

autumn & the smell
of wood fires pervades the air,
while here & there the
stuff of smoke seems to lend a
slight substance to the sun-beams

you can see that they're
not quite entirely all there
dancing together
to oldies-but-goodies with
that "special people" élan

⊕

last night I saw the
slowest falling star ever —
falling not shooting:
sort of like a spurt of fire
come to a final dribble

⊕

see the back-lit plumes
of pampas-grass shining there
in afternoon sun,
their flurries of bright silken
tassels tickling the fickle wind

the rocks prescribe the
route of the gath'ring river,
plus the voice it takes
on as it makes the song most
meet at each rough encounter

⊕

the river's ripples,
the bent arcs of the tall reeds,
succumb to the same
circumstantial forces: this
concurrence of wind & tide

⊕

even the little
bumps & ridges in the path
cast long shadows at
this hour of the afternoon,
in such tangential sunlight

her eyes bright turquoise,
her figure slim, she tends bar
just beyond the reach
of me & Jim, who go on
with our chat . . . about all that

⊕

the last light's later
here high on Spider Mountain,
where the trail reaches
its first highest point & the
sun goes on with its streaming

⊕

the sudden cry of
a rare bird rides the air of
this cool afternoon
upstream beside the river —
here where just plain ducks don't go

somehow the center
of that spider-web shines like
a golden bead there
in the day's final sunlight —
a glint from a fly's belly?

⊕

I hear a dog's tail
thumping the floor right outside
my door, telling me
something with iterative
gestures of canine gladness

⊕

shadows of cyclists
rolling along the levee
sweep across the reeds --
sun low in the western sky --
ducks in afternoon preening

full moon down the track
to the east — ling'ring sunset
glow in the west — like
fiery flamingoes mixed with
coral persimmons all ripe

⊕

a desiccated
dead rat lying on the gray
gravel beside the
railroad-tracks evokes mem'ries
of long-lost Fred Nettlebeck

⊕

peeling puff-balls, I
see that delicacies so
exotic deserve
such special patience, just as
it is with you, ma chérie

DOUBLE TANKA

I haven't grown tired
of being in this long green grass
between the levee
& the river, right where the
tall reeds in the wind begin

a grove of many
small willows gives me shade &
company as I
await understanding &
ready myself to mark it

⊕

the lovely light beige
velvet hills at Bradley seem
to have eschewed oaks
so that their soft smooth sides might
play out their entire beauty

. . .

does ev'ry place have
a "Joe's Place"? Paso Robles
does, & there it is,
just as we pull out of this
little oak-loving city

the dark fruit of these
old "Trees of Peace" lie scattered
all along the walk;
a flurry of talk rises
from the busy noon patio

. . .

two busts, of Pauling
& of Einstein, greet all guests
who climb the curving
marble stairway toward their rooms,
then that gilded Chinese hutch

⊕

the river wears a
mirror-like stillness as the tide
& current come to
a common understanding —
which is to say: no flow go

as such it maps the
skyline beyond the levee
on the other side;
& if you look close, you can
see ripples in the palm-trees

they squirm in their seats,
kicking & swinging their feet
not very close to
the beat of the opening hymn . . .
they'd rather be in a gym

those chairs are empty
now that they're in their classes
missing the talk of
the visiting minister 'n'
his squawking old woman's voice

⊕

a flurry of birds
appears as I look up &
out the window: stretched
out southbound just past the
dark tips of those tallest firs

smaller than crows, &
heading not sunward, but down
toward the torrid south
where winter's already done
with its snow-falls & flurries

a lone crow, playing
with the air — what's provided
by way of lift &
carry, as it flaps & then
glides now, ceaselessly circling

of course there's backdrop:
the tall redwoods on all sides —
one of which is there
so close to where the crow is,
it might decide to land there

⊕

this old Hollywood
juniper twists around it-
self as it stretches
its four massive trunks farther
into the welcoming sky

there beneath the tree
I find a shiny penny
& quick sense a chance
for metaphor meet to meet
our national situation

so far as I know,
poison oak wields no smell — yet
it could be hell if
it got too close to your nose …
or rubbed on you from your clothes

a tricky little
herb-like thing at first that then
becomes a vine which
climbs to sheathe these forest trees
so no one dare embrace them

⊕

in this lingering
later light — not yet last — I
settle again here
among the sorrel & ferns
to await what a bard earns

I s'pose it's mostly
vision: an expanded view
on whatever this
world pretends — this rich, massive
amalgam of sheerest sense

arriving at my
usual perch by the river,
I spot a brown duck,
but not the brood she tends there,
till they're all on the water

they got away so
fast I couldn't count them — those
fresh new fledgling ducks,
clumped up against their mother,
heading for some other shore

⊕

high in a burnt-out
redwood, a woodpecker pounds
out a xylophone-
like irregular rhythmic
sequence of resonant sounds

on a closer tree,
a small tit or chickadee
climbs poking along
little by little up the
rough, raggedy, red-brown bark

the dead red lizard
up ahead on the highway
turned out to be a
strip of redwood-bark — a frag-
ment of imagination

I had lizards on
my mind since I'd just seen one
about to cross the
road & shooed him back into
the grass just past the asphalt

⊕

even a pencil
thin madrone-branch wears the deep
beauty of its kind:
bark so smooth it bares a sheen
akin to that of satin

where else in these woods
can you find such a fine hue?
that rich reddish brown . . .
almost the color of the
legendary roan stallion

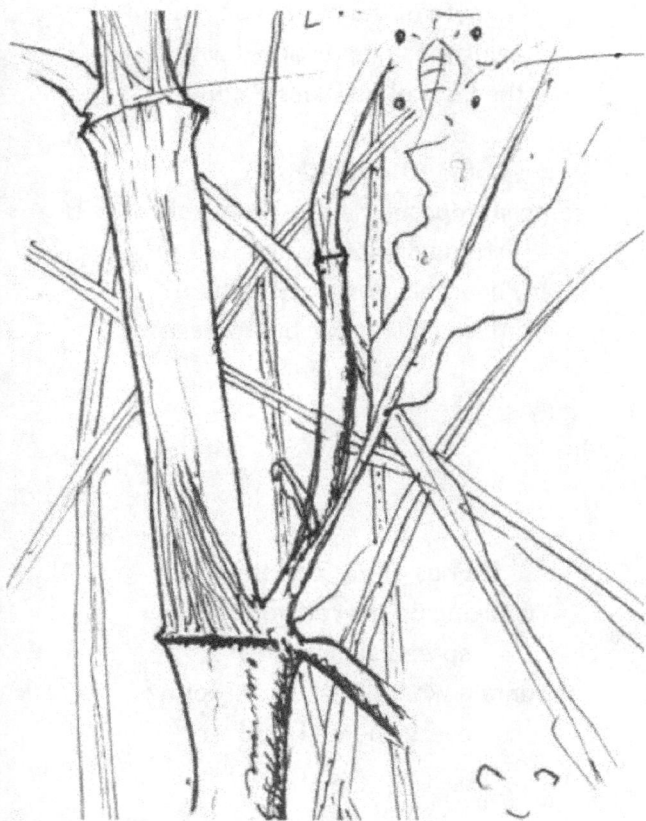

redwood-stumps become
druid thrones in the mind &
myth of the bard, who
melds the legends of old with
the facts of his place & time

some stumps are soft, &
some stumps are hard — what sort of
stump do you need now,
my dear mister wand'ring bard?
from which to more broadly see

⊕

sounds of my foot-steps
trudging up the redwood duff
spread all over this
mountain where fresh sorrel springs
up everywhere like clover

it's not clover, of
course, but a similar sort
of little green plant,
with its three heart-shaped leaves &
its gregarious attitude

these just beyond teen-
age weenies in their speedy
little cars seem to
think they're the living stars of
some movie yet to be made
. . .
yet at highway's edge
what's left of the river's sound
bespeaks those wild rocks
down there taking its waters
where they'll decide they should go

⊕

my sky is not your
sky, for mine has many more
patterns & labels:
wonderful magical names,
similarly eternal

you may consult your
infernal statistical
tables, but I have
come to know the actual
mythical stuff of the stars

it's hard to count cows
moving over their pasture,
some slow, some faster,
blocking one's visual alley
& lousing up the tally

yet yesterday I
tried it when I spied a herd
of Holsteins having
dinner in the waning light . . .
I don't think I got it right

⊕

a bird who lives at
river's edge has got to learn
to dip & glide to
get beneath those over-hanging
willow-boughs that shade its nest

. . .

we assume each bird
knows best as to how to place
its home: an avian
feng-shui — with which we humans
may not in each case agree

with wings like that they
glide in so low & slow just
above the rippling
surface of the river, then
settle on a broad sand-bar

this the generic
m.o. of that long-leggèd
great blue heron, who's
been here in these riverine
precincts twice this afternoon

⊕

the first roses seem
to've rushed to the top of the
bush & haven't stopped
pushing even farther up
into the gushing sunlight
. . .
in the hush of the
early morning, their pink shapes
shine like bright beacons
before the dark backdrop of
live oak-trees there beyond them

another tall &
willowy blonde walks past &
enters the café:
her long legs & slim arms
are just her visible charms

. . .

I'm sure there's more there
than might meet even the most
careful eye – for one,
her face, which, turned away, I
couldn't see as she passed by

⊕

the teal-headed male
attends upon his mate as
she tips & dives down
into the river; then he
tips & dips there beside her

their pair of fluffy
butts now poke up in the air
above the water
like two just-steamed artichokes
art'f'ly fashioned from feathers!

druid fastnesses
engender the vision &
embolden spirit . . .
just to sit in these quiet woods
fills me with a calming awe

who is to say that
we are more or less wise than
these tall old redwoods?
what if they can't write or talk?
they do all right just standing

⊕

't's like slicing the tails
off legless & headless mice
as I trim & dice
the beets before I put them
into the sweet-pickle-jar

. . .

lumplets of honey
sweeten my natively "plain"
container of other-
wise smooth & creamy yogurt,
which now can count as dessert

just the light of the
sky on the highway when that
spectral shape appeared
crossing before me: I flashed
on the deer as she vanished

. . .

the question may not
be whether a being has
Buddha-nature or
Christ-nature, rather whether
it produces scrumptious plums (!)

⊕

this edge of Mud Bay
scintillates in the sunlight
as the signs of life
of subterranean things
come burbling to the surface

. . .

thousands of tiny
pockets of water shine up
from the brown muck like
the swarms of stars that glow in
the precincts of the Archer

that portrait stares out
at us with eyes made of ink:
printed circles that
affect us with their quite spare
& simple similitude
. . .
so many other
faces do not show so much
staid resolution —
something which perhaps will not
fade the way printer's ink does

⊕

I caw up at the
chorus of crows that has now
settled in the tall
trees just across the river,
adding my dulcet tenor
. . .
suddenly they're all
airborne in a great swirling
confusion of caws
& squawks among flurries of
black wings bearing them elsewhere

the dip who writes these
dippy songs could surely use
some deep'ning! it's clear
this ain't no Cole Porter crowd;
he's funny, but over proud

. . .

your taste's gauged by what
you'll put up with as "art" or
comp'tent performance –
the aesthetic comp'ny you keep;
the openings through which you peek

⊕

31 years since
Mount St. Helens blew its top –
that chthonic titan
still tall enough for snow, yet
so much taller years ago

. . .

the noise it made was
prob'ly heard as far away
as nearby Portland,
& even rattled Seattle,
& homes in old Tacoma

green-headed ducks head
south to'rd the mouth of the river
going with the flow
their metallic sheen brilliant
in this late afternoon sun
. . .
she wore light green sleeves
that time one time in the park;
a lime-green it was,
& now years past I recall
the blond fuzz of her body

⊕

down the street giggling,
the rain's stoppt, umbrella's furled;
she pokes it up at
a flow'ring cherry-tree, makes
a shower of petals fall down
. . .
through tissue-thin clouds
the afternoon sun presses
its bright intentions,
such as: to later light up
these swarms of cherry-blossoms

I thought I might say:
"Fare thee well, ne'er-do-well!" but
there was abs'lutely
no one there to say it to,
so I kept it to myself

. . .

when she spoke 't'was like
soft whispers from a deep well,
& then at the end
there was no one who knew or
could tell if she'd jumped or fell

⊕

now the tall clover
towers over the lower
shorter grasses that
carpet parts of this sandy
little peninsular ledge

as close to the edge
of the river as the shade
& topography
allow – where now I follow
current whims into small poems

a red-winged blackbird
calls from atop a willow;
I look up at once
to see him & to know him
& to watch him flap away

. . .

willow-branches wave
against a clear, pure blue sky;
not even a bird
to disturb that: they're all down
here hunting on the river

⊕

I turn myself on.
Heighten my sense of myself.
This erotic me.
My lovely anatomy.
To touch, not merely to see.

. . .

I am rather sick
of my self-sufficiency –
my stark solo life.
Better old marital strife
than this new-found loneliness?

dragonflies still here
even in late September,
& I remember
my late wife, whose chief totem
these astounding creatures were

. . .

blue-tailed damselflies
stay busy in the fresh grass
beside the river,
while their larger cousins glide
over its still glossy mirror

⊕

I dreamed I almost
took my wife's Scrabble-set as
I left our marriage
but saw her name on the box
& took it back in the house

. . .

after Scrabble we
would repair to her sun-porch,
there to snuggle &
dream in those hopeful precincts
where the moon-beams were falling

so what's the answer,
merganser? & she rose up
& flapped her wide wings
as she & the male with her
glided on down the river

what might we make of
a wordless gesture so well
timed that it seemed a
response to my question; could
it mean to "believe the birds"?

⊕

huge hoppers, piled high
with yellow pulp, pull past as
I dance to the chimes
of the faithful crossing-gates;
then box-cars, box-cars, box-cars

& finally that spate
of opaque-walled freight abates
& gives way to the
diaphanous empty cars
for hauling fresh-sawn lumber

on a bus window,
the darkened number of the bus
like a line of four
black swans sailing directly
toward me: 2222

my view's foreshortened,
so their necks are very long –
longer than the necks
of the four white swans above
the logo banning smoking

⊕

splashing & burbling
from a small rapids right there,
bridging the river
with its roughly rounded stones,
none of them a true boulder

downstream, yes! three big
rocks, one of them huge – no doubt
a boulder – though this
is now the river proper,
& no longer Boulder Creek

the raven saw the
postage-stamp & then cawed out
"FOREVER"? what could
they possibly mean by that?
maybe we should have a chat

.   .   .

"poetry" begins
with Poe — as if you didn't
know; & ends with "try" —
always apt admonition;
find your own ammunition (!)

⊕

a new kind of bird
has just occurred in the same
old river precincts:
distinct from ev'ry other
sort I've ever seen or heard

yellow in its hues,
but mostly subdued grays &
other dark colors;
another of its ilk perched
in a willow while it swam

"Eat the rich!" some say:
i.e. turn them with too much
green into a rich
nutritious soilent green,
then proceed to serve them right!

ah! what a night of
feasting that might be: when those
with the least get to
play hosts, raise toasts, & down roasts
of those who once had the most!

⊕

the red-wing blackbirds'
stay around these parts involved
a part of May plus
some of June; but now they seem
to have gone away — so soon!
. . .
a blue dragonfly
zig-zags through the tall reeds, then
zips out over the
river where here & there small
pieces of sky are shimm'ring

that white butterfly,
flutt'ring among the reeds &
grasses, once did not
know it would become just that —
or did it somehow know that?

can you imagine
the surprise on the face of
the caterpillar
who woke up to find that it
had become that butterfly?

⊕

a pelican flaps,
then glides for a while — those wings
stretched out wide, but still . . .
till that sinking-feeling hits;
then it's flap-flap once again

what has brought it in
from the ocean, I can't know,
but watch its slow rise
over the river & far
beyond in the pure blue sky

something — who knows what —
caused those gulls to all at once
vacate the sandbar
at which they'd all assembled:
gregariousness on the wing

in other words, birds
of a feather not only
gather but also
fly off together, taking
that principle to the sky

⊕

put a Ferrari
under your Xmas-tree, a
red one, like in that
Beverly Hills showroom view —
or maybe an XKE

the palm-trees, sheathed in
lights to half their height along
the street, look like tall
illuminated loofas
in regimental array

after the storm's passed,
araucaria-branches stretch
along the sidewalk, blown
a whole half block north from that
magnificent tow'ring tree

long ling'ring clouds stretch
across select patches of
sky now limpid blue —
¡ay! ¡qué lindo el cielo ya!
so clear & clean & lovely!

⊕

the first oxalis-
flowers have raised their bright heads
among still budless
golden poppies, whose lacelike
leaves spread widely left & right

a scraggly straggler
sow-thistle foists its own spare
blooms a ways away,
proffering a second yellow
within that broad bed of green

three young girls clamber
all over the lone statue
outside in front of
the library: Emily
Dickenson showing a book

to a boy & a
girl who sit in rapt response
to whatever words
the misspelled mistress may be
sharing from those bronze pages

⊕

suddenly a huge
charcoal gray "3" appears on
the back of a man's
pure white tee — no more room there
for any further digit

the music sounds like
didgeridoos played under
water to snare-drum
accomp'niment from above
through the nearby coastal air

out of the corner
of my eye I spot a black
& white cat creeping
up the bank toward me, but
it's just the shimmering creek!

a small patch of sky
reflecting off the ripples,
with the silhouettes
of dark tall trees breaking up
those bright lines of wavering light

⊕

this fiery Rorschach
bespeaks some secret hidden
realm where phantasmic
figures cavort & gambol
among proprioceptive flames

they claim to have cracked
some distant star wide open
for all our minds to
finally see the bright chaos
that hides behind creation